FASHION IN
THE 1920s

Jayne Shrimpton

SHIRE PUBLICATIONS

SHIRE PUBLICATIONS
Bloomsbury Publishing Plc

PO Box 883, Oxford, OX1 9PL, UK
1385 Broadway, 5th Floor, New York, NY 10018, USA
Email: shire@bloomsbury.com

SHIRE is a trademark of Osprey Publishing, a division of
Bloomsbury Publishing Plc

First published in Great Britain in 2013 by Shire
Publications

Transferred to digital print-on-demand in 2019

Printed and bound in Great Britain.

A CIP catalogue record for this book is available from the
British Library.

Shire Library no. 774.   ISBN-13: 978 0 74781 308 8

Jayne Shrimpton has asserted her right under the
Copyright, Designs and Patents Act, 1988, to be identified
as the author of this book.

Designed by Ken Vail Graphic Design, Cambridge, UK.
Typeset in Perpetua and Gill Sans.

www.shirebooks.co.uk
To find out more about our authors and books visit our
website. Here you will find extracts, author interviews,
details of forthcoming events and the option to sign-up for
our newsletter.

COVER IMAGE
Youthful couples wearing short flapper dresses and sleek
evening suits dance at a fashionable nightclub in this
illustration from The *Sphere*, 1927.

TITLE PAGE IMAGE
A well-dressed family gathers in the photographer's studio
for a group portrait in 1923. Their clothing and hairstyles
reflect early-1920s fashions and their respective ages.

CONTENTS PAGE IMAGE
A lithograph by Raoul Dufy illustrates feminine
summer dresses for the *Gazette du Bon Ton* in 1920.
The barrel-shaped female silhouette was typical of the
beginning of the decade.

ACKNOWLEDGEMENTS
I am grateful for the help and support of several individuals
and organisations in the production of this book, especially
those who have generously contributed images from their
family archives or professional picture collections. In
particular I should like to thank:

Fiona Adams, pages 51 (top), 61 (top); Rosie Ansell,
page 54 (bottom); Linda Culm, pages 14 (right), 40
(bottom); Pat de Haer, title page; Claire Dulanty, pages
34, 47 (right), 58 (top left); Jon Easter, page 18; Julie
Guernsey/1860-1960.com, pages 9 (top), 15 (top),
19 (bottom), 24 (bottom right), 25, 29 (bottom),
40 (top left, top right), 41 (top, bottom left), 42 (all),
55 (left); Julian Hargreaves, page 21; Maureen Harris,
contents page, pages 7 (bottom right), 15 (bottom),
16 (bottom), 37, 52; Mary Evans Picture Library, cover
and pages 4, 7 (bottom left), 8, 9 (bottom), 31, 35 (top),
44, 48; John Mason, page 33 (top); Punch Cartoons, page
32 (bottom); Pauline Robertson, page 54 (top); The Royal
and Ancient Golf Club of St Andrews/The Bridgeman Art
Library, page 58 (upper right); Katharine Williams, pages
19 (top), 22 (top), 24 (top), 50 (right), 51 (bottom),
55 (right).

All other images are from the author's collection.

Shire Publications is supporting the Woodland Trust, the UK's leading woodland conservation charity, by funding the dedication of trees.

Robes pour l'été 1920.

CONTENTS

INTRODUCTION

THE 1920s are seen as an era of liberation, modernity and progress, characterised by a decline in formality and traditional values, a more open-minded, cosmopolitan outlook, advancing technology, vibrant art and design movements, a rise in commercial culture and popular entertainment and growing interest in sports. All of these factors played a significant role in defining British fashion during this formative period of our history, at the dawn of a new age.

Life for everyone in Britain was profoundly and irreversibly affected by the momentous events of the First World War. Social upheaval and the loss of half a generation of young men undermined the rigid class hierarchy and challenged many conventions that had underpinned the old order. The 1920s are often termed the Roaring Twenties, with reference to the major metropolitan centres of the developed world. In the decade following the war, American, Continental and British cities including London, Manchester, Liverpool and Birmingham experienced rapid industrial growth, accelerated consumer demand, higher aspirations and significant changes in lifestyle for many. Poor families still struggled in squalid conditions, yet many workers benefited from new employment opportunities and enjoyed a higher standard of living than their parents and grandparents. The increased use of motor cars, telephones, electricity, wireless sets and phonographs visibly demonstrated technological progress and, whilst not all could afford modern vehicles and appliances, there was a growing sense of modernity. Despite social and economic inequalities, few living through the 1920s were untouched by the dynamic spirit of the era, and all looked forward to a brighter future.

THE JAZZ AGE

Enthusiasm for entertainment during the 1920s expressed release and the desire for pleasure and escapism after the atrocities of war. The rise of music and film and the emergence of new stage and screen role models encouraged a relaxation of conventional attitudes and started to shape the tastes and aspirations of the post-war generation. The period is sometimes labelled the

Opposite:
This decadent scene set in a bar in 1925 illustrates the impact of lively jazz music on urban lifestyle, popular culture and fashionable dress, particularly from the mid-1920s onwards.

Above left: Cover image from *Vogue*, 1929. The 1920s are seen as an age of modernity. Although not everyone enjoyed the latest gadgets, increasing use of the telephone was one of many visible signs of technological progress.

Above right: Characters in silent black-and-white movies of the 1920s wore striking costumes and heavy make-up. Exotic couture gowns designed for Hollywood actresses influenced international fashion and inspired a taste for glamour.

Jazz Age, as a result of the tremendous influence of jazz music on popular culture by the mid-1920s. Jazz arrived in Britain from America and was heard at home on the wireless, played on phonograph records and danced to in new dance halls and nightclubs. Its improvised rhythms inspired a revolutionary, syncopated style of movement that contrasted sharply with the sedate waltz and foxtrot – still favourites with the older generation – while the adulation of female and black African-American jazz artists overturned existing gender and racial taboos. Jazz, regarded by the conservative as immoral and decadent, a dangerous threat to established values, was used by 1920s youth to rebel against tradition. Like all popular music trends ever since, it inspired new, controversial modes of dress: the radical modification of constricting clothes and the adoption of short 'flapper' dresses were bold and thrilling fashion statements.

MOVIE-STAR STYLE

Media and public attention also focused increasingly on film during the 1920s, and especially American movies. The UK film industry lagged behind, but Hollywood movies reached British audiences, and visiting new Art Deco picture palaces to watch the latest releases was becoming a popular form of entertainment. Until the end of the 1920s, black-and-white films were also silent and relied on strong visual effects to convey mood, character and plot, so powerful sets, costumes and make-up were of supreme importance. Many contemporary fashion designers worked in cinema, creating new costumes or lending gowns from their collections, and as film productions increasingly utilised alluring outfits, so designers met the challenges of working in a colourless medium by experimenting with tonal variations and introducing textured fabrics such as lamés, sequins and feathers. The pioneering female costumes, hairstyles and cosmetics developed for cinema had a significant influence on both haute couture and mainstream fashion, while early gangster-type movies also impacted on male youth styles in Britain.

ART DECO

Throughout the 1920s, fashion followed the development of Art Deco, a cosmopolitan and eclectic aesthetic movement in vogue broadly between 1909 and 1939, which peaked after the First World War. Art Deco displayed stylised motifs and shapes deriving from national traditions, folk art and ancient civilisations and was strongly influenced by early twentieth-century avant-garde art, chiefly the work of the Fauves and Cubists in Paris, the Futurists in Italy and Russian Constructivists. It affected all aspects of contemporary visual culture: architecture, the decorative arts, textiles and fashion, the fine arts, film and photography. By the 1920s, a very close collaboration was established between artists, illustrators and dress and textile designers, who created extraordinarily diverse and striking fashion images, garments and accessories.

Art Deco influences on fashion in the early- to mid-1920s embraced a love of eastern exoticism, rich fabrics and vibrant colours – opulent, theatrical features deriving from many different sources: the imagined Orient of Léon Bakst and the Ballets Russes, who had taken Europe by storm before

Below left: This vibrant scene from 1925, depicting a Chinese lady perusing brightly printed fabric swatches, is designed in the Cubist style. The whole image exemplifies the eclectic, diverse nature of the Art Deco aesthetic, which influenced dress throughout the 1920s.

Below right: Artists and fashion designers worked closely together during the 1920s. Georges Barbier, who created this stunning image, 'Au Revoir' (1920), displaying exotic haute couture evening wear, was among the decade's most celebrated fashion illustrators.

the war; Chinese and Japanese animal and floral motifs and Japanese kimonos; ancient Egyptian symbols, hieroglyphics and jewels, following the archaeological discovery of Pharaoh Tutankhamun's tomb in 1922; African tribal art, and traditional Russian dress details. Russian style was especially pronounced in the early 1920s: following the Bolshevik revolution of 1917, many Russian émigrés joined French fashion couture houses and helped to popularise eastern European 'peasant' embroidery as a post-war substitute for ornate materials and the combination of fabric and fur in fashionable daytime and evening garments. By the mid-1920s, the more fanciful aspects of Art Deco style were giving way to sparer, Cubist-inspired linear and geometric designs, elementary forms and bold contrasting colours. Although evening dress remained luxurious, daywear was becoming more streamlined, sporty and functional, new minimalist garments echoing the purer lines of late-decade Art Deco.

NEW TECHNOLOGY AND READY-TO-WEAR

A major theme of dress during the 1920s was the expansion of fashion. The social elite still set new trends and boasted the most extensive, indulgent wardrobes, but opportunities of acquiring affordable, stylish clothing were expanding for all: the wealthy and privileged classes would no longer have an exclusive monopoly on fashion. The urgent wartime demand for millions of standardised military uniforms to be produced had necessitated a rationalisation of the British garment-making industry, and afterwards the new economies and improvements progressed: machinery was updated, larger and more efficient factories were established and the system of breaking down clothing production into separate operations was advanced. Improved manufacturing

Right: This photograph, c. 1920, shows women sewing at machines in one of the many garment factories established during the First World War and the 1920s. This period saw the beginning of mass-produced clothing for women.

Opposite, bottom: Woolworths was one of the cheap chain stores that expanded throughout Britain, bringing a wide range of affordable dress-related articles to ordinary people. This caricature of a shopper whose £10 completely emptied the store dates from 1929.

processes and more factories meant that larger quantities of machine-made clothes could be produced, the growing simplicity of female dress throughout the decade also aiding the mass-production of women's ready-made garments. At the same time, synthetic textiles, chiefly artificial silks – or 'art silks', as they were known until the late 1920s – were refined and came into wider use. Coarse, shiny viscose rayon and acetate or 'Celanese' were initially considered vulgar materials, but as production improved, rayon and other man-made fabrics became an

acceptable, economical substitute for pure silk and were used for many dress items in the lower and middle ranges of the market, from ladies' stockings, underwear and clothes, through children's garments to men's ties.

Above: During the later 1920s, synthetic fabrics were improved and became an economical substitute for pure silk. This 1920s floral print rayon robe is styled to resemble an expensive silk garment.

The rise of mass-market British fashion during the 1920s was facilitated not only by new technology, but also by the spread of early multiple stores selling inexpensive ready-to-wear garments and accessories. Notably, Woolworths expanded dramatically in Britain, opening a new store every seventeen days by the mid-1920s: these 'Threepenny and Sixpenny stores' sold factory-made goods at rock-bottom prices, including many dress-related items from 'notions' (haberdashery) and paper patterns to underwear,

shoes, jewellery, children's school clothes and toiletries. In addition, new costumiers or 'guinea gown shops' selling special gowns for dance halls were springing up, while one of the earliest high street fashion chains, C&A, opened branches in London (1922), Liverpool (1924), Birmingham (1926) and Manchester (1928). Such popular retail outlets greatly encouraged consumer demand and helped to bring what were once considered luxuries within the reach of more ordinary working people.

Reasonably priced manufactured garments reduced the need for the second-hand articles that traditionally served poorer people, although hand-me-downs from one child to the next were common in large households; impoverished families still acquired cheap, low-quality goods from street markets, or used clothes from dealers. Better dress items were sometimes pawned from Monday until Saturday, when they were redeemed for wear again on the Sunday. Clothing clubs helped those on low incomes to save for essential items and, as a last resort, there was the ragman, with his handcart of diverse cast-offs, or charities that would supply basic clothing needs.

Home-dressmaking boomed in the 1920s. A paper pattern to make this picturesque dressing gown could be ordered from the *Daily Mail* newspaper in March 1921.

DRESSMAKING AND KNITTING

Making garments was an economical way of acquiring clothing and, although home-made clothes lacked the status of shop-bought articles, home dressmaking boomed during the 1920s. Many women owned traditional hand or treadle domestic sewing machines and some acquired modern electric machines when their homes gained electricity. Home dressmaking was also encouraged by the growing simplicity of women's and children's styles, as it was now becoming possible to run up garments relatively easily, without advanced sewing skills. Paper patterns also became more reliable and convenient: for example, in the early 1920s, Butterick introduced an enlarged and improved instruction sheet, which was much clearer and more user-friendly. Paper patterns were widely available in Britain, by mail order or from shops, and were also included as magazine supplements. Special-interest sewing and needlecraft magazines proliferated and these featured free garment patterns as well as sewing tips, articles and instructions for making and embroidering fashionable accessories.

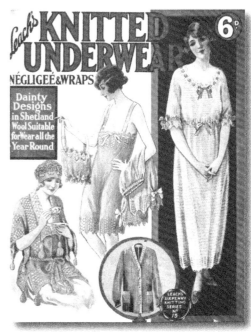

Hand-knitted garments also became a major feature of dress in the 1920s. During the war, women had sent knitted 'comforts' to the troops and afterwards cosy knitwear became popular for men, women and children, especially for winter. Knitting patterns produced by companies such as Weldon's, Leach's and Jaeger provided instructions for knitting everything from underclothes and baby outfits to jumpers, cardigans and sets of matching hats, mufflers and gloves. Some knitwear designs displayed fashionable contrasting colours, and patterned pullovers in the Fair Isle style were much in vogue. The introduction of various novelty yarns gave knitting a further boost and crochet work was also admired: popular magazines like *Fancy Needlework Illustrated* included both knitting and crochet patterns.

Many different factors impacted on British dress during the 1920s, individuals' experiences varying widely, reflecting their personal circumstances. The remainder of this book considers the key fashion themes during this decade of monumental change. Using written sources, oral accounts and contemporary visual images, ranging from fashion illustrations and paintings, through newspaper and magazine advertisements to family photographs, the following chapters examine fashions for women, men and children and the special clothing worn for evening occasions, weddings and sport.

Above left:
Many sewing and needlework magazines were published during the 1920s. This edition of *The Needlewoman* included a pattern for making a flapper frock and instructions for embroidering evening shawls.

Above right:
Knitwear became popular after the First World War. These early 1920s knitting patterns demonstrate how even nightwear and undergarments like camiknickers, vests and slips might be knitted at home.

WOMEN'S FASHIONS

WHEN WE THINK of 1920s fashion, we generally picture the decadent 'flapper' with easy manners and morals, who wore short dresses and make-up, cut her hair, smoked, drank and drove fast cars and danced – the fun-loving, modern 'bright young thing'. The decade was certainly a dynamic era for women: major legislative changes awarded them crucial divorce and child custody rights and in 1928 all British women over twenty-one gained electoral equality with men. Having assumed important working roles during the war, a significant number of single females now earned independent incomes and were developing a sense of liberation and greater confidence. Many women, especially the younger generation, embraced exciting new ideas about personal presentation, following the latest fashions in clothing and accessories, hairstyles and cosmetics. Innovation was a key theme of the decade, yet to focus exclusively on bold trendsetters and extreme fashions would be an oversimplification: female dress throughout the 1920s was far more complex and diverse than the archetypal flapper image might suggest.

After the war, affluent ladies of leisure resumed the custom of changing their dress throughout the day for different occasions, aided by personal ladies' maids. In high society, different outfits were needed for motoring and sports, social calls, formal lunch and afternoon events, evening functions and simply relaxing indoors. Paris remained the source of new fashions and wealthy British ladies visited Parisian couture houses to purchase original models (designs), while, for the slightly less prosperous, Paris fashions were replicated in the design rooms of large department stores and by upmarket dressmakers. Yet times were changing: reliable domestic servants were becoming scarcer following the war and many single women throughout society were seeking careers or more meaningful roles in which dress could no longer encumber, but had to complement a demanding schedule. Close followers of fashion didn't necessarily want fussy, time-consuming garment fittings, preferring ease, style and variety, while working-class women desired economical, practical and attractive clothes. The development of a more convenient,

Opposite:
This illustration
from *Vogue*,
November 1926,
demonstrates
the growing
importance of
cosmetics during
the 1920s and
the new lipsticks
twisting up out of
a metal tube that
encouraged the
trend of applying
make-up in public.

Above Left:
This brisk fashion illustration from *Vogue* (1927) expresses youth, confidence and freedom. While perhaps an idealised image, more modern comfortable clothing certainly gave many women a new sense of liberation.

Above right:
Affluent ladies, who owned many outfits for different social occasions, visited Parisian couture houses for the latest fashions. This stylish evening dress, designed by Worth, was illustrated by Georges Barbier for *La Gazette du Bon Ton*, 1922.

modern female wardrobe was a major trend of the 1920s and was achieved through the progressive simplification of dress as the decade advanced – a rejection of formality and multiple layers, in favour of comfort and a lighter, more natural effect.

1920s DAYWEAR

At the beginning of the decade, the fashionable silhouette was loosely tubular or slightly barrel-shaped, continuing post-war modes, while hemlines were worn to calf length. For daywear, tailored yet relaxed suits were popular, a dressy or plainer blouse worn with a skirt and matching loosely belted thigh-length jacket. One-piece day or afternoon frocks featured plain or pleated skirts, a choice of necklines and either long, three-quarter length or short sleeves. Fashionable materials ranged from woollen fabrics and gabardine, through velvet and crêpe to lightweight cottons, georgette, silk and taffeta, according to the season and the occasion. For household chores and jobs like factory work, a printed cotton overall or pinafore was slipped on over the day dress. For outdoor wear, capes and roomy blanket coats with wide sleeves and shawl collars were fashionable, as were belted coats and raincoats with long reveres or with a high neckline, collars and cuffs often edged with fur in winter. Fur was a significant fashion feature of the 1920s and was becoming affordable for more ordinary women. Full-length winter fur coats, deep fur garment trimmings and accessories such as wraps and necklets were created from various furs, including seal, coney, skunk, beaver and monkey.

The idealised early-1920s image was one of modest, girlish femininity, the language of contemporary garment advertisements including the terms 'dainty', 'pretty', 'becoming' and 'picturesque'. However, the fashionable line rapidly grew narrower and straighter and increasingly obscured the contours of the female figure. The natural waistline lowered to a dropped waist, which shifted attention to the hips, the hip area of garments often accentuated further with a sash, embroidery or other ornamental detailing. Flat, straight dresses also offered a perfect canvas for artistic Art Deco motifs and consequently many striking materials were produced, using

Above:
This delicate white cotton batiste dress, ornamented with blue silk thread, expresses the early-1920s vogue for Russian and Eastern European peasant-style embroidery.

Left: This striking dress by Paul Poiret, illustrated in *La Gazette du Bon Ton*, 1922, shows the fashion for bold materials, patterned with stylised Art Deco motifs.

Above left: Garments were
calf-length at the beginning of
the 1920s and the fashionable
silhouette was loosely tubular or
'barrel-shaped', as seen in these
clothing advertisements from
Alfred Day and Derry & Toms
of Kensington (*Daily Mail*,
8 March 1921).

Above right: Belted raincoats
based on Paris models, full-length
fur coats and stylish fur
accessories were among the
fashionable outdoor garments in
Barkers of Kensington's 1921
spring sale (*Daily Mail*, 8 March
1921).

Left: A formal embroidered
organdy picture dress by
Lanvin and straight-cut afternoon
frock by Doucet, illustrated in
La Gazette du Bon Ton, 1922,
show the variations in early
1920s fashionable style.

By mid-decade, fashionable day dresses had grown shorter, hemlines ending just below or around the knee, as seen in this illustration from Art - Goût - Beauté, 1925. Notice the bold fabric and dropped waistline, a sash accentuating the hip area.

This 'four generations' family photograph taken in 1925 demonstrates the widening gap between the appearance of younger women and the elderly, who often wore conservative floor-length black dresses well into the 1920s.

embroideries, appliqués and stylised floral or geometrically patterned prints. The new interest in printed textiles encouraged the creation of fabric designs to suit the shape of the finished garments, an idea deriving from Japanese kimonos that gave rise to some of the most ravishing dresses of the period. Oriental and other exotic influences were also evident in exclusive pieces, designed and worn by the avant-garde, for example, woven or embroidered garments incorporating ancient Egyptian symbols. Meanwhile a more widespread interest in Eastern European folk art inspired dresses and blouses ornamented with Russian-style embroidery or 'peasant' features.

A notable exception to the new plain, straight line was the so-called 'picture dress', which had a pronounced waistline and a full, sometimes hooped 'infanta' skirt, reviving the romantic silhouette of the 1915–16 'war crinoline'. The designer Jeanne Lanvin promoted the picture dress, which was intended mainly for formal weddings, garden parties and graduation balls: it appealed especially to debutantes and older women who preferred its traditional, feminine effect; some favoured the style well into the 1920s, gradually dropping the waist and shortening the length, keeping pace with broader fashion changes.

Around mid-decade, a significant shift occurred in the styling of clothes. In 1924, high fashion dictated that day dresses and skirts become shorter. As with any major fashion innovation, many ordinary women did not adopt the revolutionary new length for another year or more, but, by 1926, most young and even some middle-aged women were wearing their hemlines around knee-length, revealing more leg than ever before. Conversely, very elderly and conservative ladies accustomed to more substantial modes disliked the daring new fashions and, like Queen Mary, who kept to pre-war styles for the rest of her life, retained their sober black, floor-length Victorian-style garments throughout the 1920s. Now that fashion increasingly favoured youth, the disparity in dress between different age groups expressed strikingly the widening generation gap.

FLAPPER STYLE

The shortening of hemlines in the mid-1920s was accompanied by an exaggeration of existing fashions and a further paring down of dress. Responding to growing interest in sport, jazz music, energetic dancing and the more angular lines of the evolving Art Deco aesthetic, the admired female figure now became even more slender, youthful and boyish, and clothing grew increasingly scanty – not only shorter, but narrower. With the new lean, androgynous silhouette, the familiar 1920s 'flapper' style was born – an image sometimes called the *garçon* look. Contemporary fashion illustration also changed radically around mid-decade, discarding much of its soft, romantic imagery and becoming bolder, more linear and glossy, its stylised, elongated figures promoting the new streamlined fashions. Outerwear reflected the changing lines of fashion, coats becoming shorter and more fitted, while tailored suits for work and smart daywear attained a neat and business-like appearance, the masculine effect enhanced by the vogue for teaming the trim jacket and knee-length skirt with a plain blouse and tie.

Materials in primary colours, plain or woven with stripes, geometric designs and large floral motifs, expressed the love of clean lines and bold patterns. For summer, simple sleeveless shifts were all the rage, although narrow-hipped day dresses were sometimes enlivened by a deep V-neckline with sharp reveres, a softer, rounded Peter Pan collar, a soft neck bow, or by asymmetrical detailing. The most elaborate daywear, reserved for formal afternoon events,

Above right:
A slender, androgynous look characterised youthful *garçon* fashions of the mid- to late 1920s. For smart daywear, a trim suit, worn with a masculine shirt and tie and neat cloche hat was all the rage, as seen in this family snapshot, c. 1929.

Right: This knee-length black-and-white day dress demonstrates the love of bold geometric fabric designs during the later 1920s, although the soft silk chiffon material, flared sleeves and detailing at the neck add a floating, feminine touch.

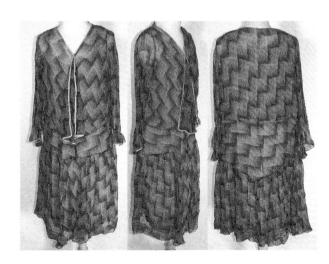

Stylish, relaxed sweater and skirt ensembles in fine jersey fabric became popular with modern women throughout society. These chic, comfortable outfits were often fashioned in muted colours, as seen in this *Vogue* illustration of June 1928.

featured cascades of drapery, wide, floating sleeves and tiered skirts, creating an elegant, fluttering effect.

Two of the most innovative and influential 1920s fashion designers were Gabrielle ('Coco') Chanel and Jean Patou: fierce rivals with similar visions who pioneered new ranges of modern daywear that were comfortable yet stylish and would suit all women. Chanel is well known for designing simple sweaters in soft stockinette jersey, encouraging the vogue for dressing in relaxed separates – the two-piece jumper and skirt suit or three-piece costume, including a cardigan. Her preferred colours were sober, almost masculine, and she often used stripes and geometric patterns, creating a chic, highly wearable style that remained fashionable well beyond the 1920s, into the 1960s. Working mainly in fine wool, her designs were expensive, but their effect was replicated at every level of the international ready-to-wear industry.

At the close of the 1920s, the stark, minimalist lines began to soften. Dress hemlines lengthened slightly and were often dipped, as demonstrated by these summer frocks worn to Richmond Park in around 1929.

Jean Patou also used jersey fabric and combined clear colours like white and navy blue to produce crisp ensembles. He recognised the need for freer yet elegant clothes for outdoor activities and successfully adapted sportswear for mainstream fashion. The society photographer Cecil Beaton described Chanel's and Patou's creations as the 'poor look': indeed the simple 'little black dress' – reportedly invented by Chanel – or the smart jersey suit could be worn by both office worker and titled lady. The quality and price of individual outfits varied, but, whether models were made up in costly crêpe de Chine or cheap rayon, the visual effect was quintessentially modern and conveyed the impression of 'democratic' fashion. Doubtless, the sense of comfort achieved from such light, easy-to-wear clothes also gave many women from all walks of life a physical feeling of liberation and emancipation for the first time.

At the end of the 1920s, the lean, minimalist lines of fashion began to soften slightly. In 1928, Jean Patou subtly lowered his dress hemlines – first at the back, then on the sides, encouraging a vogue for dipped hemlines. Finally, by 1929 or 1930, the waistline was perceptibly rising, regaining its natural position, while skirts, fitted on the hips and thighs, began to flare slightly from the knees – producing a sculptural effect that would evolve into the glamorous styles of the 1930s.

HAIRSTYLES

During the latter years of the war, some females had cut their hair short and during the 1920s, bobbed hair became synonymous with the modern, enlightened post-war woman. Not everyone was ready initially for the revolutionary new style, however: early in the decade, many women, especially older ladies, kept their long tresses, pinning the hair back; others cut only

In the early 1920s, hairstyles ranged from short bobbed hair to long hair, cut short at the sides, the length pinned back behind the head.

the side sections and wound these into a 'kiss-curl' against the cheek, the back hair coiled into a tight chignon at the nape of the neck. Nonetheless, the growing trend was for short hair, which complemented the streamlined fashionable image that was evolving, and by mid-decade many women of all ages had bobbed their hair. Amongst the ultra-fashionable in around 1922, the masculine and much talked-about 'shingle' emerged – a razor-cut immortalised by Michael Arlen in his best-selling novel, *The Green Hat* (1923). A hybrid cut known as the 'bingle' then enjoyed a brief vogue before the 'Eton crop' appeared in around 1926, a severe style slicked with brilliantine skull-like to the head, as worn, for example, by the singer and dancer, Josephine Baker. As fashions in general eased slightly by the end of the decade, such uncompromising styles and popular square bobs began to give way to more feminine, waved hairstyles.

Pond's Cold Cream and Vanishing Cream were two popular beauty aids of the 1920s, when preserving the complexion was considered important.

COSMETICS

The 1920s was an exciting and experimental decade for cosmetics. The changing needs of modern women being well recognised, there was open discussion and plentiful advice concerning beauty. Powder and rouge had for some time been readily available from department stores and chemists, and throughout the 1920s, face creams, powders and rouges for protecting and enhancing the complexion remained high on the beauty agenda. In addition, the cosmetics industry and the range of products on the market now began rapidly to expand. A significant trend was the creative potential offered by revolutionary forms of cosmetics, initially developed for the film industry. Polish-born Max Factor, now based in Hollywood, created novel forms of grease paint and powder for wearing on-screen and developed the first ever line of harmonised products: powder, rouge, eye shadow and lipstick. Reputedly, he initiated the new term 'make-up' in around 1920

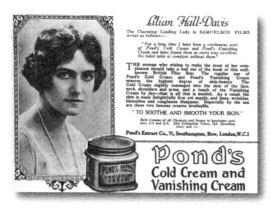

Lilian Hall-Davis

The Charming Leading Lady is SAMUELSON FILMS writes as follows:—

" For a long time I have been a continuous user of Pond's Cold Cream and Pond's Vanishing Cream and have found them in every way excellent. No toilet table is complete without them."

THE woman who wishes to make the most of her complexion should take a leaf out of the book of this well-known British Film Star. The regular use of Pond's Cold Cream and Pond's Vanishing Cream ensures the highest degree of skin-beauty. The Cold Cream nightly massaged into the skin of the face, neck, shoulders and arms, and a touch of the Vanishing Cream by day—that is all that is needed. As a result the skin is made delightfully firm yet supple, and lines, wrinkles, blemishes and roughness disappear. Especially by the use are these two famous creams invaluable.

" TO SOOTHE AND SMOOTH YOUR SKIN."

Both Creams of all Chemists and Stores in handsome opal jars, 1/3 and 2/6. Also Collapsible Tubes, 7½d. (handling size), and 1/-.

Pond's Extract Co., 71, Southampton, Row, London, W.C.1

Pond's
Cold Cream and
Vanishing Cream

and introduced pancake make-up that radically altered the nature of foundation cosmetics, his formulas henceforward forming the basis of most base make-up used by fashionable women. The growing popularity of cinema and the circulation of American movie magazines and annuals enabled British women to follow the styles and trends set by their favourite film stars. In the early 1920s the dusky, exotic look epitomised by film stars like Theda Bara encouraged some bold women to pluck their eyebrows, shade their eyelids in dark colours and use kohl to outline the whole eye. As interest in the sultry vamp effect began to wane, new movie icons like Clara Bow and Mary Pickford promoted a jauntier and more wholesome image. Eyes were widened with waterproof mascara, cheeks rouged high under the eyes, and rosebud-shaped lips accentuated with scarlet lipstick.

Martha Mansfield

Manicures also became more important during the 1920s: the development of high-gloss automobile paints inspired the introduction of the first modern nail polishes and in 1925 a sheer red nail varnish was worn by those who dared. Over the next few years, many other nail-care products were launched, with brands like Max Factor leading the way with buffing powders, lacquers and white pastes for applying under the nail tip to create an effect similar to today's French manicure. Lipsticks twisting up out of a metal tube were also introduced in the 1920s and this encouraged the vogue for applying make-up in public. Perfume manufacture also evolved during the 1920s, with new artificial ingredients appearing in the form of aldehydes (chemical compounds). Chanel No. 5, a blend of natural ingredients and synthetic floral aldehydes, was launched in 1921 – a sophisticated, romantic scent that still retains its timeless appeal.

Hollywood greatly influenced the development of 1920s cosmetics, encouraging experimentation with new forms of make-up. British women could emulate the look of film stars featured in American movie magazines, such as this issue of *Photoplay* dating from 1920.

HATS

Headwear of the early 1920s was very diverse and inventive, characterised by a vogue for asymmetrical shapes. Wartime hats had included historical and military styles like the tricorne and bicorne, and afterwards these attained more extravagant forms, made of soft fabrics and displaying irregular points, rich embroidery, tulle and feathers – all styles worn pulled down to

PARIS HATS

SMART AND INEXPENSIVE

Elegant and
serviceable
Spring Models
at special
reduced prices

Smart SAILOR of Liseret Straw trimmed band and bow of ribbon. Black, Navy, Nigger, Copper, Putty. **12/9** Box and Postage 1/6.

Smart HAT in Tagel Straw, prettily trimmed with ribbon. Burnt Terracotta, Navy, Nigger, Black, Copper, Amethyst, China Blue, Wine, Royal, Cherry and Old Gold. Special Barker Price **12/9** Box and Postage 1/6.

Useful SAILOR HAT of Picot Pedal, finished band and bow of ribbon. Madeira, Amethyst, Mastic, Putty, Royal, Old Gold, Tan, Cherry Red, Chestnut, Navy, Poilu, Terracotta. **12/9** Box and Postage 1/6. Pretty MUSHROOM HAT of Tagel Straw, crown embroidered raffia. Silver, Madeira, Mastic, Cherry, Lemon, Grey, Amethyst, Royal Blue, Red, Nigger, Burnt, Copper, Navy, Black, Gold. **12/9** Box and Postage 1/6.

Above: The deep-crowned cloche hat, pulled down low over the eyes, was worn by women of all ages during the mid- to late 1920s, as seen in this photograph, *c.* 1926–30.

Left: This Barkers advertisement displays an array of early-1920s spring hat styles, the Paris source of the fashions always cited prominently (*Daily Mail*, 8 March 1921).

Below: In the late 1920s, fashionable versions of the cloche hat were very neat and close fitting. This summer cloche of natural straw is ornamented with peach and cream silk embroidery and quilted appliqué work.

the eyebrows. Eclectic and sculptural, early-decade millinery was inspired by many sources, from oriental turbans, through Chinese *tocques*, to Russian and Egyptian headdresses. Wide-brimmed hats were also fashionable throughout the decade and presented a more dramatic or romantic appearance: gaining a deep crown, these too were worn low on the forehead and became popular for wear with light summer dresses and on the beach. The cloche is the most iconic hat of the decade, although it was not a new creation, as versions of the cloche, with its deep crown and small brim, had been worn since the mid-1910s. Acquiring its familiar neat, helmet-like appearance by around 1925, the cloche was made from various materials, felt or straw, and could be plain, or the focus for beading, embroidery, appliqué work and other decoration. The most popular hat of the mid- to late 1920s, worn by women of all ages and social classes, the cloche hugged the head closely by the end of the decade.

SHOES

With legs and feet fully on show for the first time, footwear became more important during the 1920s – a focal fashion point – and styles displayed a tremendous variety of cut, colour and decoration. Picturesque suede or patent leather Russian boots were fashionable for winter, complementing fur coats, while early-decade shoes with Louis or Cuban heels ranged from derby, oxford and brogue designs for sports and walking to dressier, bright-coloured styles ornamented with dainty bows or buckles. Already by the mid-1920s, the iconic bar shoe with a narrow strap across the instep had become a highly popular model of shoe, offering different heel heights and many different colours and materials, including reptile leather – snake, lizard or crocodile

skin – now coming into vogue for uppers or trims. In the late 1920s, street shoes grew more subtle in colour and the plain court shoe began to make an appearance.

OTHER ACCESSORIES

The long scarf draped around a swan-like neck, the ends left to trail decadently, is an accessory closely associated with the 1920s. Narrow scarves or boas and squares, worn asymmetrically about the shoulders, became must-have fashion items, whether

These 1920s flapper-style bar shoes have a black leather front, black suede back, decorative cutwork sides, and are ornamented with a silver plate buckle covering the button fastening.

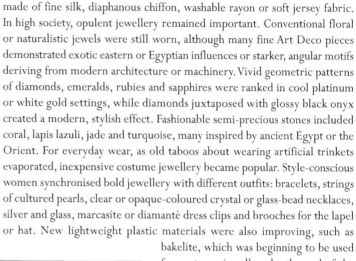

made of fine silk, diaphanous chiffon, washable rayon or soft jersey fabric. In high society, opulent jewellery remained important. Conventional floral or naturalistic jewels were still worn, although many fine Art Deco pieces demonstrated exotic eastern or Egyptian influences or starker, angular motifs deriving from modern architecture or machinery. Vivid geometric patterns of diamonds, emeralds, rubies and sapphires were ranked in cool platinum or white gold settings, while diamonds juxtaposed with glossy black onyx created a modern, stylish effect. Fashionable semi-precious stones included coral, lapis lazuli, jade and turquoise, many inspired by ancient Egypt or the Orient. For everyday wear, as old taboos about wearing artificial trinkets evaporated, inexpensive costume jewellery became popular. Style-conscious women synchronised bold jewellery with different outfits: bracelets, strings of cultured pearls, clear or opaque-coloured crystal or glass-bead necklaces, silver and glass, marcasite or diamanté dress clips and brooches for the lapel or hat. New lightweight plastic materials were also improving, such as bakelite, which was beginning to be used for costume jewellery by the end of the decade.

Bright, chunky costume jewellery became very popular during the 1920s, as seen in this *Vogue* magazine cover from 1926.

During the 1920s, many more women began to smoke publicly and ladies' cigarette cases and holders were designed in large quantities, slender cigarette holders being formed from various materials including silver, aluminium, jade, amber and ivory. The wider acceptance of women wearing make-up and applying it in public also inspired new cosmetic and vanity cases. Matching cosmetics holders comprising a cylindrical case for lipstick and a flatter compact for face powder were carried by short linked chains, while a single box ornamented with Art Deco motifs might contain separate compartments for cosmetics and a miniature comb. A popular accessory of the flapper era was the 'tango case': a compact containing powder, rouge and a lipstick, sometimes with extra card or cigarette compartments and designed to be carried ostentatiously, like a bag. The lack of pockets on slender 1920s dresses awarded bags a new significance,

particularly as many women were more active than previously, working, travelling and playing sports. Bags had to be able to carry essentials but not appear bulky, so for daywear flat leather *pochettes* or clutch bags were worn under the arm or held in the hand.

LINGERIE

Following general dress trends, a significant reduction occurred in both the quantity and bulk of female underwear during the 1920s, and this was reflected in new undergarment terminology. Old-fashioned combinations, available in various colours, styles and fabrics, were retained by some women and were considered practical for certain sports, but the wearing of narrow, unshaped garments inspired lighter and briefer underwear. Conservative and older women generally favoured conventional boned corsets and thought it unacceptable for a lady to forgo her stays altogether, but young, active women who enjoyed sports and dancing might go without, or wore either lighter corsets boned only at the sides or the new 'belt' or 'girdle' of woven elastic material. Long-line foundation garments aimed to smooth the hipline and flatten the stomach, to attain a desirable slender figure, and fashion magazines advised women to buy these two sizes too small for an even slimmer effect.

The traditional corset-cover, or camisole, gradually fell from fashion, although a narrow vest was sometimes worn, which was finely knitted from

This late-1920s illustration shows a flapper dressed in evening dance-wear and smoking, using an elegant cigarette holder – an iconic accessory of the decade.

silk, cotton or wool and trimmed with ribbon at the neck and armholes. Supportive bras with separate cups, as worn today, had not yet evolved, but flimsy bandeaux-like brassieres of fine cotton, silk, tulle or chiffon with narrow straps were worn, well-endowed ladies reportedly flattening their bosom with bandages. The full-length 'Princess petticoat' was later called the 'Princess slip' and finally the 'slip' – a simpler term for what eventually become a straight, shift-like garment, worn as a fine sheath beneath the dress. Camiknickers, an all-in-one undergarment resembling a short slip with a divided skirt, were sometimes worn instead of a slip and separate knickers and as garment hemlines rose higher in the mid- to late 1920s, both cami-knickers and knickers became correspondingly shorter, rising higher up the thigh. Regular knickers were now often called 'knicks' – another example of a shorter name for a briefer garment.

Fine, hand-made lingerie, trimmed with embroidery, lace and appliqué work, was worn by wealthy women, the most exquisite articles originating in Paris. Pastel shades were admired, such as peach, pale pink, ivory and eau-de-Nil, although fashionable colours ranged from coral to sky blue and the daring wore black lace-edged underwear. Soft fabrics such as

This sewing pattern from 1925 demonstrates the kind of flimsy brassieres and fine slips that modern women were wearing beneath narrow lightweight clothes by mid-decade.

Model No. 150.

An elegant Corset

for the

Elegant Woman

This corset has been designed essentially for the woman of refinement who likes her corset to be the foundation of her frock. It is exceptionally comfortable in wear, being fitted with spiral boning; is very short above the waist with nice flowing lines, is fitted with four suspenders and made in sizes, waists 21—26, depth in front 15 ins., at sides 17 ins. Remarkable value... **19/11**

Write for our Catalogue "Examples of Modern Corsetry," sent post free.

Worth's Corsets LTD.

3, Hamsell St., London, E.C.1.

Left: Although modern 1920s women adopted elasticated girdles or went without a corset altogether, conservative ladies still preferred the support of traditional boned foundation garments, as seen in this advertisement from 1922.

Below: This off-white silk slip, delicately ornamented with drawn cutwork, Irish crochet and filet lace and pale pink ribbon trimmings, exemplifies the luxury lingerie worn by affluent ladies during the 1920s.

fine cambric, lawn, cotton and silk were preferred for underwear, with opaque silk, satin and shantung being especially favoured for wear beneath airy *mousseline de soie* or chiffon evening gowns. Artificial silk also began to be used. Those able to afford pure silk were snobbish about synthetic substitutes, but they offered an affordable alternative for ordinary women and gave the illusion of luxurious lingerie. With rising hemlines, legs now received more attention and ladies' stockings underwent a revolution. Traditionally, woollen or cotton stockings had been black for winter and white for summer, but now women desired fine 'flesh'-coloured stockings. Novel ranges of sheer stockings in pink, beige, fawn and tan tones were introduced, in pure silk for the affluent and in cheaper rayon. The familiar British hosiery brand name Aristoc was launched in 1924, its first advertisement in *Vogue* magazine (1926) describing the product as 'a stocking of breed and character.'

MENSWEAR

FOLLOWING THE FIRST WORLD WAR, men's clothing choices were still largely governed by established dress codes. Within the middle and upper classes in particular, it was understood that a man's appearance would reflect his age, status, the occasion, season of the year and so on, according to expectation. However, the new spirit of the age demanded a fresh approach to male fashion: as rigid social etiquette began to break down and men desired more comfortable garments, so a more relaxed attitude towards dress began gradually to evolve, along with a growing interest in contemporary style.

1920s DAYWEAR

During the 1920s, the stately black or grey frock coat that had expressed authority and tradition in the Victorian and Edwardian eras grew outmoded, an anachronism in a modern world, although some older, conventional gentlemen continued to wear the conservative frock coat. Meanwhile, the suave morning coat with sloping front edges, teamed with a matching waistcoat and pinstriped trousers, was now considered correct for formal day or business wear by the social elite, morning suits also being favoured for gala occasions and events such as garden parties, the races and weddings. While these garments all had their place, the mainstay of the male wardrobe was the three-piece suit known as the lounge suit, but sometimes called the business suit when tailored in sober colours and conservatively styled. Comprising a short lounge jacket, waistcoat and trousers, the lounge suit became increasingly acceptable during the 1920s and was widely adopted throughout society. For gentlemen accustomed to more formal dress, it offered a contemporary, easier alternative to the morning suit, while the average working man wore his three-piece suit on virtually every occasion – for work, on the football terraces, in the pub, to church and to weddings.

English tailoring was considered superior throughout the fashionable world and Savile Row remained the epicentre of bespoke tailoring, although few could afford the elevated prices of prestigious Savile Row establishments.

Opposite:
This stylish image from 1927 demonstrates the snappier men's fashions of the lat 1920s. Typical features are the looser trousers with knife-edge creases, double-breasted jacket tailored with sharp lapels and jazzy 'co-respondent' shoes.

Many other tailors provided a quality service at a local level during
the 1920s, however, and most gentlemen continued the tradition
of having their suits custom-made from their chosen cloth and to
a unique pattern created from their body measurements, to achieve
the best fit. Those with high sartorial standards and a personal sense
of style shunned ready-made garments, even though men's suits
had been successfully mass-produced since the nineteenth
century. For ordinary workers with limited time and money,
there was a growing range of decent off-the-peg suits
from menswear stores such as Austin Reed, who launched
their first high quality ready-to-wear collection in 1925.
Meanwhile other high street tailor/retailers like Montague
Burton were offering affordable 'made-to-measure' suits
for as little as fifty shillings – an intermediate option,
provided garments based on standard patterns in a
limited choice of materials that were then altered and
made to fit the customer's measurements. The best
quality men's shirts were also custom-made; otherwise,
shirts and small articles such as underwear were bought
at traditional men's outfitters or, more economically, at
one of the multiple stores catering for a mass market,
such as Woolworths or C&A.

SUIT STYLES

Following pre-war lines, the early 1920s three-piece suit was
slender in style and the colours of suiting materials generally sombre
– black or greys, browns, beiges and blues. Tweeds were popular for
winter, while flannel was preferred in warmer weather. The typical
lounge jacket was hip-length, commonly single-breasted and made with
moderate lapels. Trousers, often tapered, were high-waisted and secured
with braces or a belt; sharp creases were coming into vogue, while narrow
hems that typically measured just 17 to 19 inches were beginning to acquire
turn-ups, except on formal pinstriped trousers. The fashionable length for
trousers was short, around ankle-length, so that a man's socks showed
above his shoes, unless he wore boots or spats. A matching waistcoat
completed the suit and a traditional watch chain might be suspended across
the waistcoat front, the watch concealed in a pocket, although the
wristwatch offered a more modern method of time-keeping. Shirts of a
plain colour such as blue or grey were popular with manual workers;
striped shirts with a white collar were fashionable for business wear,
although white prevailed and the white linen 'boiled shirt' with a stiffly
starched front panel was correct for formal day wear. Detachable starched

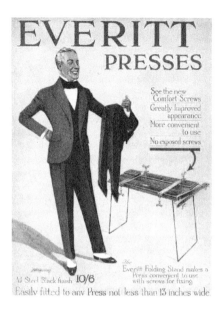

EVERITT PRESSES

See the new
Comfort Screws
Greatly Improved
appearance
More convenient
to use
No exposed screws

The
Everitt Folding Stand makes a
Press convenient to use
with screws for fixing

All Steel Black finish **10/6**
Easily fitted to any Press not less than 13 inches wide

Above: Men's trousers were often tapered and worn rather short, with narrow turned-up hems in the early 1920s, as seen in this advertisement from 1924. Some gentlemen also wore spats over their shoes at this time.

Right: Wide 'Oxford bag' trousers represented a radical new fashion that was mocked in the popular press, as seen in this *Punch* cartoon, 1925.

rounded collars remained common immediately after the war, although shirts with more comfortable un-starched collars steadily gained favour. Yet, despite this modern trend, 'white-collar' workers – a term widely used during the 1920s – were still expected to wear formal, heavily starched collars and even the traditional winged collar was worn for various occasions.

Over time the cut of men's garments altered and by the later 1920s new suits were looking snappier, with looser, knife-edge creased trousers and more shaped, double-breasted jackets with broader, sharper lapels. Clearly the time was right for a general change of style and the mood of innovation was expressed most dramatically in the radical new fashion of 1925 – longer, baggy trousers that flared to 24 inches or more at the hem and were known as 'Oxford bags'. The precise origins of wide Oxford bags is still uncertain: reputedly they were devised by Oxford students for wear over their golfing knickerbockers, which the university had banned for lectures in 1924, and certainly they were first popularised in Britain by Oxford undergraduates. The younger generation naturally took to the new trousers and other extreme fashions more enthusiastically than their elders. For example, in the late 1920s, young urban working-class men evolved their own distinctive style for visiting

ANOTHER BLOW FOR OXFORD.

dance halls and jazz clubs: wide bell-bottomed trousers with one-inch turn-ups, gangster-style 'Stetson' hats, short belted overcoats and so-called jazzers' haircuts.

THE COMPLETE IMAGE

It was important that every male outfit consisted of the correct component parts, such as the right type of tie and style of hat, if the wearer did not want to look out of place. A necktie remained an important dress accessory during the 1920s. The dignified pre-war Ascot cravat might still accompany formal morning dress, while bow ties remained popular, even for ordinary day wear; otherwise a long knotted tie prevailed and was often rather narrow. The best ties were of silk, Macclesfield silk being considered superior, although rayon was a cheaper substitute and sturdier woollen or tweed ties that would not spoil in the rain were adopted for country wear. With colour and design now becoming more important, ties were sometimes patterned with bold Art Deco motifs or lively dots or checks, although more restrained ties were plain or diagonally striped, often expressing school, college, club or regimental colours.

Hair was worn short and neatly styled, either centre- or side-parted or combed back smoothly over the head. Style-conscious young men, emulating the decade's favourite male movie star, Rudolph Valentino, used oil or brilliantine for sleek, glossy hair. Most young men now favoured a modern-looking, clean-shaven face, although the older generation might still grow a moustache or, very occasionally, a beard. Hats were always worn outdoors and gradually the bowler hat eclipsed the traditional top hat for formal day or business wear. Meanwhile, stylish felt hats became increasingly popular – either the semi-formal homburg, which could replace the bowler when teamed with the lounge suit, or more casual fedora or trilby hats with a creased and pinched crown, introduced from America. Tweed or cloth caps were worn for country and sporting activities, the

Above: Ties in the 1920s were typically rather narrow in style and made in various designs, colours and fabrics. This restrained tie of black, grey and green tweed would have been suitable for casual country wear.

J UDGED by style, quality and wear, a STETSON gives you the finest hat value obtainable— a perfect blend of flawless materials and beauty of finish.

Illustrated Stetson Booklet containing list of Agencies will be forwarded on request.

JOHN B. STETSON CO.
Offices and Showrooms (Wholesale):
70 New Bond St., London, W.1

STETSON HATS
Styled for Young Men

Left: Smart-casual felt hats like the fedora and trilby were influenced by American styles. As seen in this 1925 advertisement, Stetson hats were available in Britain by the mid-1920s and were popular with fashionable young men.

flat cap also remaining the characteristic hat style of the working man. Some thugs who roamed inner-city streets and frequented local dance halls famously sewed razor blades into the peaks of their flat caps, adding a menacing dimension to an otherwise innocuous fashion. Straw boater hats were still worn in summer, but the style was becoming outmoded and by the end of the decade had given way to the fine straw panama hat, shaped rather like the trilby.

The war had encouraged more comfortable footwear, ankle-high boots like the front-lacing derby now being worn mainly by the older generation. Lower-cut laced shoes became established as the modern choice, black calf oxfords or brogues being usual in town and brown shoes for informal country wear. Spats – light-coloured wool or canvas coverings for the instep and ankle – were popular early in the decade, but were later worn chiefly with the morning suit. As spats became outmoded, two-toned shoes with boldly contrasting panels – usually black and white or tan and white – came into vogue, a bold style that some considered too brash. However, the fashion-conscious Prince of Wales (later Edward VIII) admired two-tone 'co-respondents', as they were called, and also wore suede or 'reversed calf' shoes, widely considered the unmistakable sign of a 'cad'.

Men's underwear evolved during the 1920s, gradually following the trend toward lighter, briefer undergarments. The Victorian long-sleeved

This photograph, taken in Ireland in 1920, demonstrates the range of men's hats worn during the 1920s, from felt fedoras and trilbies to flat cloth caps. Shirt collars and tie styles also varied widely.

This cartoon of 1929, suggesting a futuristic device to help gentlemen get dressed, shows the brief singlet vest and shorts that modern men wore as undergarments by the late 1920s. Sock garters were used particularly with evening attire.

The cloth cap, styled wide above the ears in the 1920s, was the typical working man's everyday hat, as seen in this 1921 photograph of a Brighton & Hove Albion v. Norwich football match.

This advertisement from H. J. Nicoll, c. 1929, shows men's outerwear: left and centre are Chesterfield coats, worn for town or business wear with the formal top hat or bowler; right is the more casual Raglan, teamed with a felt hat.

woollen or cotton vest and ankle-length drawers ('long-johns') or all-in-one combinations were still popular, especially with the older generation, although the modern, enlightened man progressed to short-sleeved vests or sleeveless 'singlets' and shorts. Socks were often held up by sock garters, especially the silk socks worn with evening dress.

LEISUREWEAR

Despite certain advances, men did not enjoy the same sartorial freedom as women during the 1920s. For weekend wear, a striped blazer or plain or checked tweed sports jacket and flannel trousers ('flannels') became fashionable; off-white flannel trousers were sometimes worn in warm weather. Wide knickerbockers or plus-fours were also an informal or sporting option, often teamed with a knitted pullover, but a shirt and tie was still *de rigeur*: there was no real provision for comfortable, casual leisure wear, especially easy-fitting, lightweight summer clothes. For inspiration, Britain increasingly looked to America, where dress was more colourful and relaxed, the Prince of Wales being a great advocate of the modern, freer styles developing across the Atlantic. Critics of contemporary British dress regarded men as still being imprisoned in unnecessary layers of stuffy garments: the Men's Dress Reform Party, formed in 1929, campaigned for healthier men's clothing, but even their most basic aims were not fully realised until shorts and open-necked sports shirts became widely accepted in the 1930s.

For weekend leisurewear, men were still expected to wear a shirt and tie. A tweed sports jacket and flannel trousers were a popular combination, as seen in this 1922 fashion plate from the *Gazette du Bon Ton*.

EVENING DRESS

THE MOOD OF EFFERVESCENCE following the war, the rising popularity of jazz music, craze for dancing and vogue for exoticism and luxury inspired 1920s evening styles that were among the most alluring fashions of the twentieth century.

In the early 1920s, evening gowns were long, clinging and feminine, worn low on the calf or ankle-length. Depending on the occasion, bodices were short-sleeved or sleeveless, often shaped into a plunging V-shape at the back or styled along classical lines, worn off one shoulder or fastened with sparkling diamanté or metallic chain shoulder straps. Typically dresses were gathered at the hip and ornamented with a jewelled clasp or a rosette, or they featured an ostentatious bow or frill behind the waist, while narrow trains draped elegantly on the floor. Some frocks were gracefully layered, using lace, satin and net and displayed vandyked (pointed) hemlines, or picturesque petal-shaped skirts, while other gowns were fashioned from diaphanous chiffon, rich silk or sumptuous velvet, in brilliant colours or dramatic black ornamented with bright beads. Following the archaeological excavations of 1922, some evening gowns were printed with Egyptian symbols, while shimmering fabrics, theatrical sashes, exotic embroideries, appliquéd motifs and tassels reflected the enduring influence of the mystical Orient and the Ballets Russes on evening wear throughout the decade.

By the mid-1920s, evening wear was evolving and beginning to express the energy of the newly popular Charleston and other lively jazz dances. Slender, short, square-shaped dresses were secured on the shoulders by narrow straps, and skirts featured undulating hemlines or were slit on the sides or formed of multiple strips of material. Shimmering silks, fine velvets and gleaming silver or gold lamés, embroidered with glittering sequins, lustrous pearls, shining glass beads or glinting metallic threads reflected the light and created an effect of dazzling brilliance. Fashionable late-1920s evening colours ranged from black or white to Nile green, sky blue, orange and begonia, and extravagant feathers, long boas, layered skirts and swaying fringes all accentuated movement.

Opposite:
A sleek, narrow-strapped evening gown of shimmering material, ornamented at the hip, is accessorised with a decorative hair comb, pearl jewellery and an extravagant ostrich feather fan in this glamorous *Vogue* illustration from October 1922.

Above:
A sheer black net beaded and sequinned overdress with a fringed scalloped hemline is layered over a black silk dress with chiffon kimono-style sleeves, creating a stunning early-1920s evening gown.

Above right: This hot red flapper dance dress with vandyked hem comprises a red under-slip beneath a sheer red silk chiffon layer ornamented with glittering hand-sewn cobalt blue beads arranged in an abstract Art Deco pattern.

Right: In this illustration by Georges Barbier, 1923, a lady models a sumptuous fur-trimmed evening coat by Worth, complemented by a *kokoshnik*-style tiara and ostrich feather fan. Her companion wears a tailcoat, starched white shirt, waistcoat and formal evening accessories.

COATS, WRAPS AND SHAWLS

Ladies' evening wear of the 1920s was not complete without an opulent coat or wrap. Following the shifting styles of the period, evening coats and mantles of the early 1920s were loose and ample, becoming more fitted and streamlined around mid-decade. Coats had long, broad collars, displayed ostentatiously over the shoulders, or padded fabric, fur or feathered collars closed high around the neck. Velvet, satin or lamé coats and wraps might be lined with a contrasting material, while experimental new decorative techniques were used to dramatic effect, including lacquered designs and bold stencilled motifs. The popularity of the tango during the 1920s also inspired the wearing of large shawls of vivid hand-painted silk, richly embroidered brocade or paisley, edged with long fringes, cheaper versions being made in printed rayon. Eye-catching shawls patterned with bold floral designs were draped around the shoulders or arranged toga-like across the body.

Left:
Square-shaped, reversible and made of silk, this 1920s evening shawl is woven with pink, red, green and gold lamé threads to create a striking rose design.

Below left: This 1920s black silk velvet opera coat, hand-stencilled with a striking gold lamé leaf pattern, has a sea green velvet rolled collar and is lined with green silk velvet.

Below:
This *Vogue* image from July 1926 demonstrates the fashion for bright, floral-patterned, fringed evening shawls, draped around the shoulders or body.

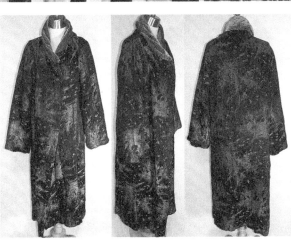

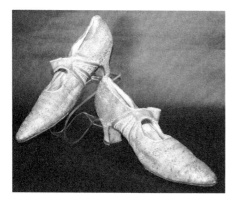

Above: These elegant flapper dance shoes with 2-inch Louis heels are made of silver lamé brocade fabric in a floral design and are lined with white kid leather.

EVENING ACCESSORIES

Bare arms and the popularity of African art inspired a fashion for 'slave' bracelets or bangles, often worn high on the arm, while strings of cultured pearls and beads and pendant jewelled or tasselled earrings all enhanced the fashionable sinuous image. Evening tiaras were prominent during the 1920s, worn for balls, weddings, state functions, elegant parties and other formal occasions. Dramatic tiaras based on the northern Russian *kokoshnik* – a traditional crown-like festive headdress, worn low on the forehead – were ornamented with lavish embroidery and jewels or were surmounted by exotic ostrich or peacock feathers. Other evening headdresses included fine beaded or sequinned flapper caps and pearl-studded or jewelled filets, turbans and bandeaux, with styles deriving from ancient cultures and the Orient.

The most exquisite footwear of the decade was reserved for evening occasions, single bars, T-bars and crossover straps securing elegant pointed

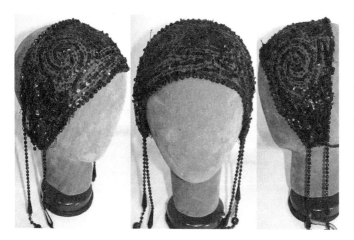

Top right: This delicate *minaudière* purse, ornamented with peach, blue, green and grey beads, has a silver plate frame, clasp and carrying chain. Inside are pink silk pocket compartments containing a vanity mirror and comb.

Left: This stylish Art Deco evening headband or cap is made from sheer black net sewn with black sequins and edged with a jet bead trim. Black strung bead loops are also suspended from the sides.

shoes to dancing feet. Shoe materials ranged from coloured velvet, silk and satin to gold and silver kid leather, lamé and brocade, the more ornamental styles embellished with hand-painted designs, jewels, sequins and pearls. Exotic embroidered or fur-trimmed 'harem slippers' were also popular for lounging indoors, worn with hand-painted silk pyjamas or loose Indian gowns. Neat evening *pochettes*, bags and purses were eye-catching and elaborate, ranging from embroidered or beaded *minaudière* purses suspended on long chains to lacquer, fabric or leather bags decorated with floral or geometric Art Deco motifs, bordered with diamanté trimming or adorned with tassels. A feather, lacquered, hand-painted or metallic lace fan completed the formal evening ensemble.

MEN'S EVENING DRESS

Men's evening dress of the 1920s remained sedate and sober in comparison with female styles. The elegant black dress or tail coat, worn with a white waistcoat, white dress shirt with stiffly-starched front panel and winged collar and a white bow tie, was considered essential for formal evening functions such as public dinners, assemblies and dances at elite venues, and was a familiar sight on the stage and screen. This traditional attire was accessorised with a collapsible top hat or 'opera hat', a long dark coat or cloak, white evening gloves, a white silk scarf and a cane. However, the more relaxed short black dinner jacket (the American tuxedo), teamed with a white shirt and black bow tie, was becoming popular for informal evening occasions including private dinners and parties, and some concerts.

Top right: The gentleman in this late-1920s fashion illustration wears traditional evening accessories: a long black coat, black silk opera hat, white silk scarf, white gloves and a cane.

Right: This plate from the H. J. Nicoll & Co Ltd. catalogue of c. 1929 shows the formal evening dress or tail coat, worn with a white waistcoat and white bow tie (right) and the more relaxed dinner jacket (tuxedo), teamed with a black bow tie (left).

THE CHILDRENS' HOUR

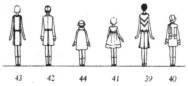

39.—Miss Thirteen-Year-Old will approve a tennis frock of yellow washing silk, designed on grown-up lines.

40.—A chic little travelling coat for a lady of seven summers, made of sand-yellow Kasha and finished with a scarf.

41.—Another charming, simple frock for the seven-year-old that looks equally well in rose and white organdi, voile or linen.

42.—A smart double-breasted redingote of golden-yellow cheviot that has been designed for the lucky little twelve-year-old.

43.—Either printed voile or washing silk is suggested for a chic model for the twelve-year-old, with practical side pleats.

44.—The small person of five will welcome a cosy brick-red woollen, smartly stitched coat as part of her travelling trousseau.

PAPER PATTERNS OF ALL THESE DRESSES, IN *THREE SIZES,* CAN BE OBTAINED FROM "BRITANNIA AND EVE'S" PAPER PATTERN DEPARTMENT.   FULL PARTICULARS ARE GIVEN ON PAGE 158.

CHILDREN'S CLOTHES

Babies' and children's clothing advanced significantly after the First World War, influenced by technological progress, shifting fashion trends and the circulation of new ideas about the mental and physical development of the young. Although wealthy parents might still buy hand-made infants' gowns from exclusive shops, or ladies with leisure time stitched exquisite baby clothes painstakingly by hand, by the 1920s, a wide range of manufactured babies' and children's garments were available from mail-order catalogues and stores, aimed largely at the middle and comfortably-off working classes. Home dressmaking using sewing machines being popular, some women made their babies' and children's clothing and there was no shortage of paper patterns and advice. Sewing manuals suggested that, rather than using their machines to copy expensive shop-bought goods, mothers should create modern, practical clothes for their children that would withstand wear and tear and would wash well.

BABIES AND TODDLERS

At the beginning of the 1920s, the conventional baby's layette retained the same number of garments as before the war: flannel petticoats were considered necessary for warmth, while flannel or stiff linen binders, wrapped twice around the baby's stomach from chest to hips, were still commonly used. Victorian recommendations concerning the wearing of wool next to the skin persisted and infants were often dressed in little woollen vests, combinations and sleep suits. Nonetheless, the general trend as the decade advanced was for simpler babies' garments and a less pronounced distinction between the 'long clothes' traditionally worn by newborns and the second 'shortening' set, and increasingly baby gowns were made of intermediate length and were roomy enough to accommodate the first year's growth.

The post-war baby boom opened up the market for baby-carriages or perambulators to all but the poorest families, and with improvements to the design of prams, it became customary during the 1920s to give babies their recommended daily 'airing' outside, ideally for several hours. Pram covers

Opposite:
Britannia and Eve was one of many popular magazines that provided paper patterns for home dressmaking in the 1920s. This plate from 1929 features several patterns for girls' summer coats and dresses.

This advertisement for Lux soap flakes, published in 1922, illustrates the kind of warm woollen underwear still recommended for infants in the 1920s.

and blankets hid the baby's lower half, so outdoor clothing now focused chiefly on the body and head: traditional long carrying capes or mantles were replaced by knitted shawls for tiny babies, while for older babies sitting up, the practical pram set was introduced, comprising a knitted or fabric matinée jacket or a short, caped pelisse-coat, worn with matching hat and leggings. Knitted 'overalls' – what we would now call 'tights' – were sometimes worn under short skirts, while versions for babies taking their first steps had 'gaiter' feet, with straps to secure them under the foot. Shaped fabric gaiters with buttons from ankle to thigh might be worn by both boys and girls aged two or three and upwards, who were still in tunics and short trousers. All manner of infants' garments were hand-knitted at home, including jerseys, dresses, kilts, tunic and knickers sets, leggings, jackets and hats, and this had a modernising effect on dress. Interesting novelty yarns like angora and 'teasel wool' were introduced and were especially popular for infants' warm outdoor hats and coats.

Whereas Victorian and Edwardian parents had lavished most attention and expenditure on their newborn babies, increasingly the needs of older babies and toddlers were recognised. The rough and tumble of young children's play began to be seen as a vital form of exercise and self-expression, and during the 1920s, there were major innovations in the dress of physically active infants. Rompers (first offered by Harrods in 1919) were revolutionary new garments – like small boiler suits, they had long sleeves, a yoked bodice and short knickerbockers. Made in plain, easily laundered fabrics, these were convenient for mothers and enabled much more freedom of movement for babies at the crawling stage and toddlers than traditional cumbersome petticoats. Several other large retailers began to stock romper suits, some offering suits styled to resemble shorts and a shirt for little boys and dresses with matching knickers for girls.

The war years and post-war period witnessed the gradual decline of the Victorian social custom called 'breeching', whereby boys discarded their baby frocks when aged around four and adopted more masculine knickerbockers. Although the convention for male and female infants to wear androgynous petticoats persisted in some families, during the 1920s

Below left: A jolly baby models the latest in fluffy woollen baby wear, demonstrating the 1920s vogue for knitting and the new 'pram set', comprising a knitted matinée jacket, matching hat and leggings.

Below: All kinds of infants' garments were hand-knitted during the 1920s. In this photograph, taken c. 1920, a toddler wears a woollen coat and hat, her leggings made with 'gaiter feet'.

ROWE
of BOND STREET

These charming original garments for children cost no more than others of less distinction—witness the competitive prices for these examples from Rowe's.

10. Linen Frock, hand-made. Saxe; butcher; periwinkle; petunia; apple; canary — trimmed white dimity. 16"-26" 47/6

11. White hair cord smock—hand-made. Smocked sky; saxe; rose; pink; mauve; green. Drawn thread work each side. 16"-26" .. 27/6

12. Dainty striped Zephyr frock. In pretty shades of green; blue; cherry; yellow; pink; mauve. Trimmed plain collar and cuffs 16"-26" 39/6

13. Mercerised jersey and knickers in fancy purl stitch. Sky/grey; sky/white; sand/sky; cherry/white; saxe/grey; lemon/white; tan/sand. All sizes 32/6

14. Buster suit, Striped Zephyr. Top trimmed solid colour to match knickers. In green; tan; mauve; yellow; cherry. 1½-5 years 39/6

15. Children's hand-made fine wool pull-over. Sky/sand/white; tango/almond/white; sand/rose/lemon; saxe/sand/white; 2-10 years 32/6

16. Rowe correct drill sailor suit, complete as illustrated.
3-6 years 32/9
7-10 years 34/9
11-15 years 37/3
Or any part supplied pro rata.

distinctions tended to be made between girls' and boys' clothing at an increasingly early age. When aged as young as two, some boys were now put into their first shorts suit; perfect for this transition was the 'buster suit', which comprised a pair of coloured 'knickers' (shorts) and a white blouse: originally the shorts were held up by fabric braces; otherwise they buttoned onto the waist of the blouse. Another means of identifying gender was through colour and the now-familiar concept of 'pink for a girl, blue for a boy' began to evolve. At the beginning of the 1920s, the reverse was common, pink being deemed a suitable colour for small boys, but rapidly pink and blue grew more closely associated with girls and boys respectively, becoming established by the end of the decade.

This Gorringes advertisement for children's clothes illustrates the new 'Buster suit', an outfit combining shorts and blouse, designed for little boys aged between around two and five years (*Daily Mail*, 8 March 1921).

"BUSTER" Charming SUIT, with knickers of soft mercerised Casement Cloth and top of White haircord muslin, smocked and embroidered by hand. Saxe/White, Pink/White, Champagne/White, Brown/White or Green/White. To fit boys 2½ to 5 years. First size ... ... **21/-** Rising 1/6 each size.

GIRLS' WEAR

Young girls' underwear usually comprised a soft, fleecy-backed cotton liberty bodice and a woollen vest for extra warmth, worn with voluminous elasticated knickers. Traditionally female children wore clothing that mirrored their mothers' dress, with certain juvenile differences. Girls' age differences were still expressed in the length of their garments, frock and skirt hemlines lengthening slightly as the girl grew older, although the custom became blurred when fashionable dress grew briefer, for girls in general began to wear shorter clothes. Early in the decade, sack-like, loosely belted frocks with wide sleeves were popular, then later on garments became narrower and simpler. Dresses with short sleeves and round Peter Pan collars or sleeveless shifts were fashionable for summer, young girls' plain linen or cotton summer dresses often ornamented with smocking, embroidery or appliqué work, while patterned fabrics might display modern geometric Art Deco shapes or more timeless floral motifs. Silk, crêpe de Chine, organdy and velvet were dressy fabrics favoured for party wear and 'Sunday best', depending on the season, although with the development of man-made fibres, pretty rayon materials became popular. The boom in home dressmaking and the tendency for smaller, more manageable families meant that many girls' clothes were made and altered at home. Following general trends, girls also wore knitted woollen garments, from sweaters and cardigans to scarves and hats.

Opposite: Upmarket children's outfitters, Rowe of Bond Street, were following new colour trends when they advertised blue jersey and shorts sets for little boys and pink frocks for girls in 1926. Note the girls' short hemlines and fashionable Peter Pan collars.

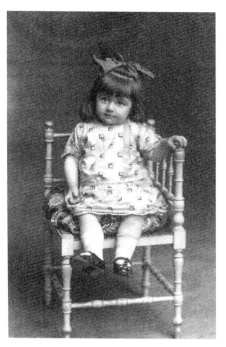

Above: This little girl, photographed in 1925, wears a short dress, its material printed with stylish geometric Art Deco motifs. Her hair is cut into a fashionable soft bob, with a fringe.

Above right: Adolescent girls adopted a youthful version of adult dress. This teenager, photographed in 1927, wears a feminine floral frock and fashionable flesh-coloured stockings, her hair styled into schoolgirls' plaits.

Along with the modernisation of clothing came simpler hairstyles and accessories for girls during the 1920s. Young girls' hair was usually cut into a short, neat bob and a fringe, although some preferred more feminine, longer hair, secured behind the head or tied into a plait or ponytail with a large taffeta ribbon. White ankle- or calf-length socks gradually superseded traditional thick black woollen stockings, extending from small children to older girls and, eventually, women (for sports), although mature 'teenage' girls, when fashionably dressed, adopted the new flesh-coloured ladies' stockings. Older schoolgirls generally wore a regulation uniform comprising a blouse, short gymslip, stockings, blazer or raincoat and hat bearing the school badge.

BOYS' WEAR

The modern 1920s boy wore undergarments comprising a short-sleeved or sleeveless singlet vest with 'knickers', the contemporary term for drawers. With the early-twentieth-century heavy woollen knickerbockers suit now decidedly outdated, pre-school boys past the toddling stage often wore a belted thigh-length tunic with matching shorts or a knitted jersey and shorts set in coloured wool or rayon. Plain hand-knitted or machine-knitted jerseys with collars and sometimes an integral matching or contrasting tie took

Left: This snapshot, taken c. 1920–1, shows a pre-school boy dressed in a belted thigh-length tunic and shorts set. His older brothers wear jerseys, the machine-knitted sweater on the left featuring an integral collar and tie – a typical 1920s garment.

Below:
Two young brothers, photographed in the mid-1920s, wear uniform-style school clothes: their blazers, flannel shorts, grey socks and laced leather shoes were probably also worn for best weekend wear.

boys through their primary school years, worn with above-the-knee shorts. The vogue for Fair Isle sweaters set by the Prince of Wales began to inspire brightly patterned knitwear for boys, as well as for men. The growing trend for garments to cross over from sportswear into regular dress was also reflected in pleated flannel trousers and woollen blazers, initially worn for cricket and tennis. By the 1920s, flannel trousers or shorts and blazers had become the regulation or unofficial school uniform for older schoolboys, the Army & Navy Stores charging between £1 and £2.10s for such a suit in 1929.

With even tiny boys now wearing shorts, sartorial distinctions between male children of different ages centred on the issue of short and long trousers. 'Longs' were usually adopted when a boy attained his early teens, an age that often coincided with his entry into the working world. Some secondary and grammar schools set a height qualification for wearing long trousers, while others insisted that even older male pupils wear shorts, to their embarrassment. Laced shoes replaced old-fashioned leather boots, and rubber-soled canvas plimsolls were widely worn for games, as well as for leisure, although boys in poorer communities sometimes went to school barefoot – a reflection of the economic hardships experienced by some families at this time.

A SPRING wedding is always beautiful, but this year it's going to be prettier still, for the white bride is no longer *the* thing, and dainty colours may be chosen. As it is tulip and daffodil time, why not a "yellow" bride? I have chosen for her this frock of yellow georgette, with pearl trimming and tassels, and given her a veil of ivory lace, held in place by tinted yellow orange blossoms. And her bouquet—why, yellow tulips, of course!

Patt. No. 922

A "crocus" bridesmaid would make a sweet "background" for a "yellow" bride. Choose the *shaded* georgette for this frock—it portrays the *flower* effect so prettily—and wear a mauve tulle veil with clumps of flowers over the ears, keeping it in position by a tinsel ribbon band. Isn't the little bouquet of many-colour crocuses charming?

Pattern No. 923

BRIDAL WEAR

TWO WIDELY PUBLICISED royal weddings in the early 1920s had a significant influence on bridal fashions. When Princess Mary, daughter of King George V and Queen Mary, married Viscount Lascelles in February 1922, she wore a traditional royal bridal dress of silver, with a court train embellished with floral motifs and an overdress embroidered with beads and pearls, her Honiton lace veil a family heirloom. A more novel bridal ensemble deriving from medieval Italian styles was worn by Lady Elizabeth Bowes-Lyon for her marriage to the King and Queen's second son, Prince Albert, Duke of York (later King George VI) in April 1923: her narrow ivory chiffon moire gown was ornamented with bands of silver lamé and seed pearls; she wore two trains, one suspended from her shoulders, another from her waist, her lace veil circled by a chaplet of white flowers and myrtle leaves.

These special occasions and the fairytale royal bridal gowns inspired a new generation of brides and helped to revive the sense of romance that had been absent from weddings during the war. Many 1920s brides chose cream or ivory for their wedding day, although soft pastel shades were also admired, such as pale yellow, blush pink and peach. Fashion favoured airy fabrics like silk, chiffon and georgette, and the more ornate bridal garments were embellished with embroidery, lace, pearls or beads. Most wedding dresses emulated the royal bridesmaids' afternoon length outfits, rather than the royal brides' long, trained gowns, and since fashionable hemlines fluctuated throughout the decade, bridal wear followed suit, set at calf-length in the early to mid-1920s and rising to just below the knee by 1926. The hems of wedding dresses were often scalloped or featured handkerchief points, while medieval influences might be expressed in long, narrow sleeves or elongated, pointed bodices. Bridal veils were usually fashioned from lace or net, and frequently they were loaned to the bride, meeting the time-honoured custom of wearing 'something old'. The veil was secured by a headdress worn characteristically low over the forehead; styles ranged from simple silver or satin bandeaux decorated with artificial flowers to tiaras or diadems of paste, diamanté or wired lace and conventional headdresses of wax buds of orange

Opposite:
These springtime wedding patterns from Mabs Fashions, 1925, recommend a bridal dress of pale yellow georgette with pearl trimming and tassels and an ivory lace veil. The bridesmaid's frock is of shaded mauve georgette with a mauve tulle veil.

In 1925, this bride wore a lace and silk or georgette dress and veiled headdress worn characteristically low over her forehead. Two flower girls wore wired caps, a distinctive 1920s style, while the groom sported formal pinstriped trousers and spats.

This bride of 1928 is hard to distinguish from her bridesmaids as they all wear white or pale-coloured flapper-style knee-length dresses, typical of the later 1920s, with wide-brimmed hats and identical accessories. The groom wears a regular three-piece lounge suit.

blossom, myrtle and pearls. Although the prevailing trend was for a feminine bridal gown and veil, some brides wore a fashionable afternoon frock or suit and wide-brimmed hat or cloche.

Bridesmaids' dresses were occasionally made full-length, but usually followed the shorter afternoon style and were typically fashioned from silk, satin, organdie, tulle or taffeta in delicate floral prints or plain pastel colours like mauve, powder blue or peach; sometimes bridesmaids wore veils too, but more usually a stylish hat and fashionable accessories. It was also the vogue in the 1920s to have an entourage of children – small, picturesquely dressed bridesmaids and, sometimes, pageboys – the more affluent the family, generally the more attendants. Little girls carrying flower baskets might wear high-waisted, puff-sleeved dresses and mob caps, emulating the historical Kate Greenaway style, while another distinctive bridesmaid accessory was the wired cap with horizontal wings that often resembled the Dutch headdress. Young pageboys often wore very fanciful outfits, such as Highland dress or eighteenth-century court costume.

Upper- and middle-class bridegrooms generally favoured a dark morning coat and grey or pinstriped trousers, with a dark waistcoat and silk top hat. Meanwhile, the average working man wore a smart three-piece lounge suit on his wedding day, accessorised with a coloured knotted tie, a contemporary hat, such as the homburg or trilby, and white gloves, in honour of the occasion. Sometimes the lounge jacket was teamed with striped trousers, spats, a shirt with a stiff winged collar and bow tie, to create a more formal appearance. Family wedding photographs from the 1920s demonstrate the variety of wedding attire worn during this decade of change and innovation.

Above left:
This exquisite 1920s wedding dress of ivory silk satin is sleeveless and features a fashionable rosette at the hip. The sheer yoke inset and tiered skirt are of net, ornamented with fine bobbin lace.

Above:
Many brides wore white bridal wear during the 1920s. This photograph from 1923 depicts a bride wearing a traditional dress with the characteristic low calf-length hemline of the early 1920s. Her veil is attached to a headdress of artificial flowers.

SPORTING STYLE

Dᴜʀɪɴɢ ᴛʜᴇ 1920s, dancing and various outdoor sports became more popular. It was now recognised that energetic physical movement could also be beautiful and there was a growing awareness of health and fitness. The contemporary fashion term 'sportswear' generally implied relaxed, comfortable clothes for leisure occasions, rather than garments worn specifically for sports. The two were closely interrelated at this time, although changing fashions, sporting progress and new technology advanced the dress worn for particular sporting activities.

MOTORING GEAR

The number of motorcars on the roads increased significantly during the 1920s, although private car ownership was not yet widespread and motoring was still chiefly considered a sport. Closed-in vehicles became more common as the decade advanced, but some were still exposed to the elements and motorists driving in open-topped models adopted special protective driving gear, similar to pre-war styles. Early in the decade, loose motoring duster coats were a common sight and warm hats were a necessity. Later, driving garments became more streamlined and with the development of competitive motor racing and more advanced sports cars, style and speed combined to produce sleek belted leather motoring coats, soft leather driving gauntlets, close-fitting caps and aviator-style goggles.

GOLFING DRESS

Golf was the most fashionable upper- and middle-class activity of the 1920s. Wide knickerbockers or 'plus fours' were fashionable for men, along with sturdy brogue shoes. The Prince of Wales, who always liked to cut a dash, set the tone as captain of the Royal and Ancient Golf Club of St Andrews with a tweed cloth cap, soft-collared shirt and tie, jazzy knitted pullover, tweed plus fours and argyle socks. Knitwear, whether hand-knitted or commercially machine-made, was already well-established for sport, but only in the early 1920s did the Fair Isle sweater, featuring bands of coloured pattern on

Opposite:
Art Deco style, sport and speed come together in this bold *Vogue* image from 1925, teaming a sleek sports car with an elongated driver wearing a fashionable streamlined jersey motoring dress, leather gauntlets, racing helmet and goggles.

a neutral background, appear on the golf course. Golfing ladies wore the usual 'sportswear' combination of comfortable sweaters, cardigans and skirts, with sturdy stockings and brogues.

Above left: These male motorists from the early 1920s, touring in an open-topped car, wear traditional protective motoring duster coats over their suits and cloth caps or tam-o'-shanter style hats.

Above: This 1927 painting of the Prince of Wales from the Royal and Ancient Golf Club of St Andrews demonstrates how he led 1920s golfing fashions with his patterned jersey, plus fours, brogues and cloth cap – a style followed by many.

Left: Female golfers wore casual 'sportswear' on the golf course – comfortable jersey separates, warm socks and sturdy brogue shoes, as seen in this *Vogue* illustration from autumn 1923.

TENNIS WHITES

Tennis enjoyed a tremendous vogue during the 1920s and glamorous summer tennis scenes were used to advertise consumer goods ranging from lawnmowers to confectionary and drinks. Men's tennis wear comprised easy-fitting long white or cream flannel trousers, a white shirt and a blazer, plain or striped in club, school or college colours (these colours were also echoed in the bands edging the V-necked pullover). Outer layers were discarded for play, although initially a formal collar and tie were usual, until open-necked shirts became acceptable later in the decade. Tennis shoes were made of white canvas, leather or buckskin and had rubber soles. Women usually wore a casual dress, or blouse or V-necked sweater and skirt, the skirt often pleated to facilitate movement. Wimbledon champions always set new standards and the French player Suzanne Lenglen, who wore Jean Patou-designed clothes both on and off the court, revolutionised tennis style by wearing a flimsy calf-length frock with short sleeves and a length of silk chiffon as a headband. By the late 1920s, following her lead and embracing wider fashion trends, sleeveless, knee-length shift-like tennis dresses were fashionable.

Right: This designer sports dress from Molyneux features a silk bodice printed with bold floral motifs and a pleated skirt. Illustrated in *Art - Goût - Beauté* in 1924, it was recommended as suitable for playing tennis.

Above: Tennis dress developed rapidly throughout the decade. By the late 1920s a sleeveless, knee-length shift-like white dress was usual, often worn with a scarf or bandeau around the head, as seen in this *Vogue* illustration, June 1927.

This advertisement from *The Sketch*, Christmas 1926, announces the latest weatherproof winter sportswear from Burberrys. Fashioned in bright colours, suits were both stylish and practical and included revolutionary female jodhpur-style trousers and breeches.

WINTER SPORTSWEAR

Winter sports were becoming more popular amongst the moneyed classes after the war. Traditionally, thick knitted jerseys, scarves, hats, gloves and socks were worn in the snow, teamed with calf-length skirts, breeches or trousers and leather boots. During the 1920s, ski knitwear became slender in style and often displayed brightly patterned designs, while breeches or jodhpur-style trousers were increasingly worn by women. Specialist outdoor clothing companies such as Burberrys were also developing new ranges of functional yet stylish water- and snow-proof winter sportswear; fashion-conscious Britons on the slopes of Switzerland modelled the latest gabardine ski suits tailored in bright, highly visible colours.

Burberry is a most protective and comfortable dress for Winter Sports. Designed by experts, Burberry models embody the latest tips and every essential for the full enjoyment of sport on snow or ice.

Burberry Winter Sports materials are porous, yet weatherproof. Warm, snow-proof, wind-proof, airylight and cool: all qualities ensuring healthful enjoyment. Finely woven, with smooth surfaces, snow never clings to Burberry materials.

Winter Sports Catalogue and Patterns of Materials Post Free

BURBERRYS HAYMARKET LONDON S.W.1
8 & 10 BOUL. MALESHERBES PARIS & AGENTS

BEACH COSTUMES

Summer holidays abroad were enjoyed by those who could afford to travel, while many working families looked forward to their annual break at a popular British seaside resort. In the early 1920s, bathing attire for women typically comprised a concealing two-piece bathing suit of heavy serge or woollen cloth. These garments later grew briefer, the dress or tunic neckline lowering, sleeves reducing to broad shoulder straps and hemlines rising, while the drawers contracted into thigh-length shorts. Yet some still found the bulky layers cumbersome and, as reservations about displaying the body's contours relaxed, the one-piece female costume with short legs became more popular – a streamlined style already adopted by competitive swimmers and sometimes called by its French term, the *maillot*. The new costumes were especially figure-hugging when cotton and woollen jersey fabrics began to be used and also acquired a more sporty appearance, with contrasting

In the early 1920s women's bathing suits were still rather modest, combining a short-sleeved tunic and thigh-length drawers or shorts, as seen in this snapshot taken in Devon, 1924. Men's costumes retained the old-fashioned vest section throughout the decade.

This illustration from summer 1929, depicting a fashionable holidaymaker wearing lightweight beach clothing, including daring beach pyjamas, was the first ever *Vogue* cover to feature female trousers worn as day wear.

white or bright-coloured trims. By the end of the decade, fashionable women's costumes were altogether more alluring, with shorter legs and narrow shoulder straps or halter necks. Meanwhile, close-fitting rubber bathing caps – suitable for newly-bobbed hair – were beginning to replace jersey turbans and rubber two-tone beach shoes were becoming fashionable.

Besides reflecting the general simplification of dress during the 1920s, one of the factors behind the modernisation of swimwear was the new vogue for acquiring a suntan: sunburned skin, once the unwelcome sign of outdoor manual labour, was now coming to symbolise leisure time and relaxation. The new trend rapidly extended from the glamorous resorts of California, Florida and the French Riviera to British beaches, encouraging the unprecedented exposure of parts of the body previously concealed. Men's costumes changed little throughout the decade and retained their traditional vest section, but women benefited from not only more liberating bathing costumes, but a whole range of stylish beachwear, now that it was customary to stay on the beach after a swim, instead of changing immediately before and afterwards. New beach garments included short dresses of taffeta or satin, worn over the swimsuit, or brightly coloured wraps of towelling or printed waterproofed silk. By the late 1920s, skimpy, lightweight holiday clothing was also evolving: backless sun tops, sleeveless blouses and new beach pyjamas for the bold.

FURTHER READING

Blackman, Cally. *One Hundred Years of Menswear*. Laurence King Publishing, 2009.

Breward, Christopher. *The Culture of Fashion*. Manchester University Press, 1995.

Byrde, Penelope. *A Visual History of Costume: The Twentieth Century*. Batsford, 1986.

Byrde, Penelope. *The Male Image: Men's Fashion in England 1300–1970*. Batsford, 1979.

Carter, Alison. *Underwear: The Fashion History*. Batsford, 1992.

Cunnington, C. Willett. *English Women's Clothing in the Present Century*. Faber and Faber, 1952.

Ewing, Elizabeth. *History of 20th Century Fashion*. Batsford, 1986.

Fiell, Charlotte and Dirix, Emmanuelle. *Fashion Sourcebook: The 1920s*. Fiell Publishing, 2012.

Lussier, Suzanne. *Art Deco Fashion*. V&A Publishing, 2003.

Niven, Felicia Lowenstein. *Fabulous Fashions of the 1920s*. Enslow Publishers, 2011.

Owen, Elizabeth. *Fashion in Photographs: 1920–1940*. Batsford, 1993.

Phillips, Clare. *Jewels & Jewellery*. V&A Publishing, 2000.

Pointer, Sally. *The Artifice of Beauty: A History and Practical Guide to Perfumes and Cosmetics*. Sutton Publishing, 2005.

Rose, Clare. *Children's Clothes*. Batsford, 1989.

Shrimpton, Jayne. *How to Get the Most from Family Pictures*. Society of Genealogists, 2011.

Wilcox, Claire and Mendes, Valerie D. *Twentieth-Century Fashion in Detail*. V&A Publishing, 2009.

Wilson, Elizabeth and Taylor, Lou. *Through the Looking Glass: A History of Dress from 1860 to the Present Day*. BBC Books, 1989.

PLACES TO VISIT

Bexhill Museum, Egerton Road, Bexhill on Sea, East Sussex TN39 3HL.
   Telephone: 01424 787950. Website: www.bexhillmuseum.co.uk
Brighton Museum & Art Gallery, Royal Pavilion Gardens, Brighton,
   East Sussex BN1 1EE. Telephone: 03000 290900. Website:
   www.brighton-hove-rpml.org.uk/museums/brightonmuseum
Fashion Museum, Assembly Rooms, Bennett Street, Bath BA1 2QH.
   Telephone: 01225 477789. Website: www.museumofcostume.co.uk
Gallery of Costume, Platt Hall, Rusholme, Manchester M14 5LL.
   Telephone: 0161 245 7245. Website: www.manchestergalleries.org/
   our-other-venues/platt-hall-gallery-of-costume
Museum of London, 150 London Wall, London EC2Y 5HN.
   Telephone: 020 7001 9844. Website: www.museumoflondon.org.uk/
   london-wall
Victoria and Albert Museum, Cromwell Road, London SW7 2RL.
   Telephone: 020 7942 2000. Website: www.vam.ac.uk
Worthing Museum & Art Gallery, Chapel Road, Worthing, West Sussex BN11
   1HP.   Telephone: 01903 221448.
   Website: www.worthingmuseum.co.uk

INDEX